The Red Rocket Pirates

Maverick

Early Readers

'The Red Rocket Pirates'

An original concept by Katie Dale

© Katie Dale

Illustrated by Elena Resko

Published by MAVERICK ARTS PUBLISHING LTD

Studio 11, City Business Centre, 6 Brighton Road,

Horsham, West Sussex, RH13 5BB

© Maverick Arts Publishing Limited February 2020

+44 (0)1403 256941

A CIP catalogue record for this book is available at the British Library.

ISBN 978-1-84886-658-4

www.maverickbooks.co.uk

Yellow

This book is rated as: Yellow Band (Guided Reading)
This story is mostly decodable at Letters and Sounds Phase 3.
Up to eight non-decodable story words are included.

The Red Rocket Pirates

by **Katie Dale**   illustrated by
Elena Resko

We are the Red Rocket Pirates!

Meet Biff,

and Jill,

and I am Peg-Leg Bill.

This is my parrot, Pip, and my ship,

The Red Rocket!

Look! We can sail fast!

Eek! That was TOO fast!

Quick, shut the door!

We look for dinner.

13

Eek! That is a SHARK!

Quick, let him go!

We look for land.

I can see land!

Eek! That is a big rock!

Quick, get off the ship!

Can we get to the land?

Eek! A crab! Quick, get it off!

23

We dig for gold.

Is it full of gold?

Yes! It is the best gold of all!

Quiz

1. What is the parrot's name?
a) Chirp
b) Pip
c) Jill

2. What did the pirates catch?
a) A shark
b) A whale
c) An octopus

3. What did the ship crash into?
a) Land
b) A big rock
c) A shark

4. We ____ for gold.
a) Swim
b) Look
c) Dig

5. What kind of gold did they find?
a) Money
b) Gems
c) Choc

Turn over for answers

Book Bands for Guided Reading

The Institute of Education book banding system is a scale of colours that reflects the various levels of reading difficulty. The bands are assigned by taking into account the content, the language style, the layout and phonics. Word, phrase and sentence level work is also taken into consideration.

Maverick Early Readers are a bright, attractive range of books covering the pink to white bands. All of these books have been book banded for guided reading to the industry standard and edited by a leading educational consultant.

To view the whole Maverick Readers scheme, visit our website at

www.maverickearlyreaders.com

Or scan the QR code above to view our scheme instantly!

Quiz Answers: 1b, 2a, 3b, 4c, 5c